W9-DCH-985

NOT FOR RESALE
This is a Free Book
Bookthing.org

How Your Media Choices Make You Feel

Jean C. Lawler

RED CHAIR PRESS

Experience Personal Power books are produced and published by Red Chair Press

Red Chair Press LLC   PO Box 333   South Egremont, MA 01258-0333

www.redchairpress.com

 FREE Lesson Plans from Lerner eSource and at www.redchairpress.com

Publisher's Cataloging-In-Publication Data

Names: Lawler, Jean C.

Title: Experience media : how your media choices make you feel / Jean C. Lawler.

Other Titles: How your media choices make you feel

Description: South Egremont, Massachusetts : Red Chair Press, [2018] | Series: Experience personal power | Interest age level: 007-010. | Includes a glossary and resources for further reading. | Includes index. | Summary: This book helps children to make thoughtful media choices, including knowing when to "unplug."

Identifiers: ISBN 978-1-63440-376-4 (library hardcover) | ISBN 978-1-63440-380-1 (paperback) | ISBN 978-1-63440-384-9 (ebook)

Subjects: LCSH: Digital media--Psychological aspects--Juvenile literature. | Emotions--Juvenile literature. | Choice (Psychology)--Juvenile literature. | Self-control--Juvenile literature. | CYAC: Digital media. | Emotions. | Choice (Psychology) | Self-control.

Classification: LCC HM851 .L39 2018 (print) | LCC HM851 (ebook) | DDC 302.23/1--dc23

LCCN: 2017948353

Copyright © 2019 Red Chair Press LLC
RED CHAIR PRESS, the RED CHAIR and associated logos are registered trademarks of Red Chair Press LLC.

All rights reserved. No part of this book may be reproduced, stored in an information or retrieval system, or transmitted in any form by any means, electronic, mechanical including photocopying, recording, or otherwise without the prior written permission from the Publisher. For permissions, contact info@redchairpress.com

Illustrations by Nathan Jarvis.

Photo credits: Kristen Ball 16 (small photo); Courtesy of the Author 24; iStock Cover, 1, 3–16 (large photo), 18 (small photo), 22, 23; Scott MacNeill 17–20

Printed in the United States of America

0518 1P CGBF18

Table of Contents

Getting Started:
Think About You

Which do you like to do the most: watch a movie, read a book, play outside?

How often do you use a cell phone?

What is your favorite TV show, movie, or video game?

Tune In to Media

What do you wonder about when you hear the word media?

Perhaps you think of television, cell phones, and music players. Or video games, computers, and the Internet. Other words for media are technology and electronic **devices**. Believe it or not, books and newspapers are kinds of media, too.

There are many different kinds of media. Media includes anything that gives us information, or messages. Sometimes it is words on a page. Other times we see pictures or hear words. Videos and movies give us moving messages!

Media is everywhere. Inside and outside, day and night, 24/7. We can **connect** to different types of media anytime: messages on a cell phone, websites on a computer, pictures on a camera, maps on the car dashboard, ads on TV, the PA system in a school, books from a book club.

People connect for different reasons: to talk with someone, to learn something, to entertain themselves. It's handy to be able to call someone on the phone. It's easy to look something up on the Internet. And it's fun to watch a silly movie.

You can use media to help make your life easier and happier. Cameras help you see and talk to relatives who live far away. Texts let you tell friends you are thinking about them. Music makes you feel good.

It can be hard to get away from media messages. It's fun and once you are playing or watching it might be hard to stop. Sometimes you might forget you can do other things like draw, build a puzzle, or just talk to someone.

Notice how you feel after using certain media. Playing video games in the morning might make it hard to focus in school. Reading a book before bed might help you get to sleep. Listening to a certain song might make you feel like dancing!

You can learn a lot about yourself by **tuning in to** the media you use each day and how it makes you feel.

Make Sense of Media

There are so many ways that media can be important in your life. It helps you stay in touch, it helps you learn, it helps you have something fun to do. You can learn a lot about yourself by paying attention to your media choices.

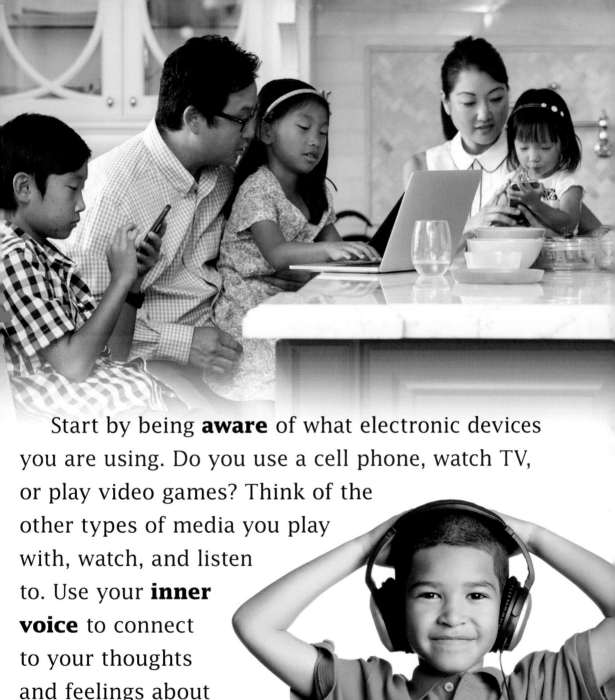

Start by being **aware** of what electronic devices you are using. Do you use a cell phone, watch TV, or play video games? Think of the other types of media you play with, watch, and listen to. Use your **inner voice** to connect to your thoughts and feelings about what you're doing. Notice what's going on with your body.

Paying attention to your thoughts and feelings while using media is a healthy thing to do. Let your inner voice help you **be present** with your emotions as you play, watch, and listen. Are you feeling excited? Calm? Happy? Afraid?

Technology can affect your feelings and your actions. When you feel a certain way, you might act out your feelings. If you see violence in a game, you may think it's okay to hit someone. A movie about rescuing animals may make you want to adopt a cat. Be sure to check in with your thoughts and feelings.

Power Point

Your power comes from taking care of yourself. You increase your personal power by breathing fresh air outside, eating well, being quiet for a few minutes each day, and making your own decisions about when to use media.

You get **personal power** when you pay attention to your inner voice while using media. This power helps you think about what's happening to you when you play, watch, and listen. It helps you make a decision that's right for you. You might decide to watch another show or turn off the TV.

Sometimes it's okay to choose no media at all! You can use your personal power and decide to do something else.

Media can be useful to you in school! You can make a video for your report. You can use Skype to visit other schools. You can write to an author to say how much you liked a book.

Technology is helpful and fun and can be in good **balance** with other activities like running and jumping, reading and writing, singing and playing.

Sometimes using media becomes a habit. But you can think about it and make different choices for yourself.

Unplug for a little while. Pick a time during which you will not use any electronic device. That means not watching TV, playing video games, listening to your music player, or anything that plugs in or uses batteries.

If you feel the urge to pick up your video game, you need to choose something else to do: go outside to play, take out a board game, or read a book.

Start a journal where you write about what it was like to make different choices about technology.

On the first line, write what you wanted to do. On the second line, write what you did instead. On the third, write how you felt when you did something different.

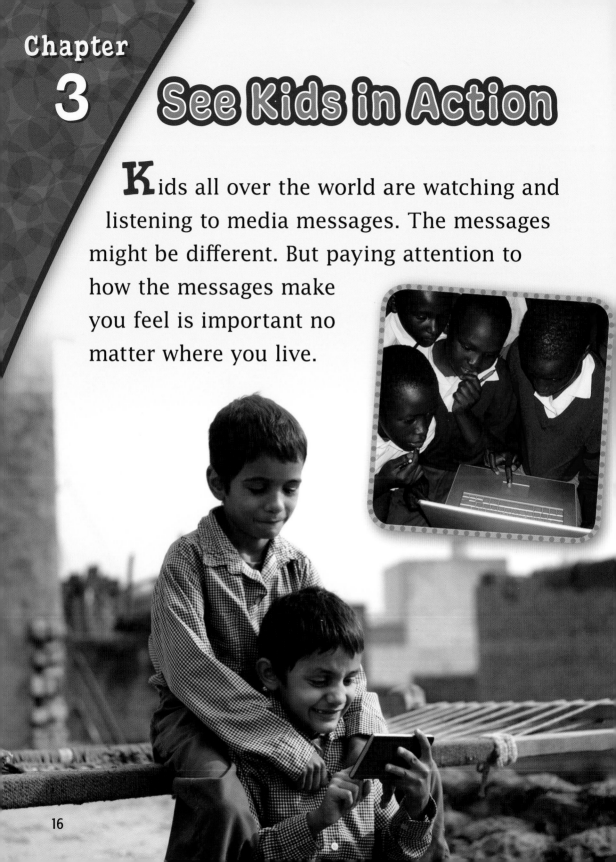

See Kids in Action

Kids all over the world are watching and listening to media messages. The messages might be different. But paying attention to how the messages make you feel is important no matter where you live.

At the Russell Byers Charter School in Philadelphia, Pennsylvania, kids learn about media and how watching and listening to it affects them. They also use technology tools to create their own media messages.

17

The kids at this school pay attention to four kinds of media. Print media is what you read. Visual media is what you watch. Audio media is what you listen to. Interactive media is on a device you watch or play with. They talk and write about what they like and dislike about each kind of media. Noticing their preferences helps the kids build their personal power.

Some media messages are real and some are make-believe. These kids discuss the difference between what is true and what's imaginary as they watch and listen. Knowing the difference helps them understand more about their own lives.

Some media messages, like TV ads, make you want to buy things. At this school, kids discuss how some media messages can affect what they want and the way they feel. They use their inner voices to notice if the media messages they see make them feel like singing, throwing something, laughing, going shopping, or something else.

Kids at Russell Byers choose their own "back-up person," who helps them while they are using media. If they don't understand something, if they don't feel safe online, if they are stuck, the "back-up person" is there. Having a human to connect to during media time helps kids build their personal power.

Moving On:
Taking Action Yourself

Get involved in learning more about how media is made.

Create a video yourself. Ask your teacher if you can use the school equipment.

Become more mindful of what's around you by taking photographs.

Make a sound recording as you walk around your school or neighborhood. How many different sounds can you identify?

Record yourself reading a book to share with younger children.

Look for new things to do, other than use media: go for a hike, cook something, make up a song.

Keep using your journal. Write and draw about how different kinds of media make you feel.

Glossary

aware: noticing or paying attention to something

balance: when parts are equal

be present: to notice what is happening right now

connect: to join together

device: tool made for a certain purpose

inner voice: thoughts and feelings you have in your own mind/body

personal power: the ability to think and do things that help you succeed

tuning in to: to focus on something

For More Information

Books

Cordell, Matthew. *hello! hello!* Hyperion, 2012.

Droyd, Ann. *If You Give a Mouse an iPhone*. Blue Rider Press, 2014.

Oberschneider, Michael. *Ollie Outside: Screen-Free Fun*. Free Spirit Publishing, 2016

Smith, Lane. *It's a Book*. Roaring Brook Press, 2010

Zuckerberg, Randi. *Dot*. Harper, 2013

Web Sites about Media Use

http://pbskids.org/dontbuyit/

Note to educators and parents: Our editors have carefully reviewed these web sites to ensure they are suitable for children. Web sites change frequently, however, and we cannot guarantee that a site's future contents will continue to meet our high standards of quality and educational value. You may wish to preview these sites and closely supervise children whenever they access the Internet.

Index

About the Author

Many media sources were used in the creation of this book!
Jean Lawler did research on the internet, called people on
her cell phone, watched videos, and wrote using her computer.
She appreciates the conveniences of technology but also
likes to go for walks outside, sit and talk with friends, and do
mindful meditations.